r:
Letters Between
J.R. and Miss Kim

Poems by Jeannie Hoag & Kyle McCord

© 2011 Jeannie Hoag & Kyle McCord

Published by Gold Wake Press

ISBN 13: 978-0-9826309-9-0

Cover design: Brian Mihok

GOLDWake Press

Letters

Letter to Miss Kim (The Only Day) / 7

One:

Letter to J.R. (Every Day the Little Arts Are Dying) / 11
Letter to Miss Kim (This Disaster Area) / 12
Letter to J.R. (The Three Storms) / 13
Letter to Miss Kim (Renew Each Day with a Match) / 15
Letter to J.R. (If One Could Forget Katmandu) / 16
Letter to Miss Kim (To Stand and Face the Face of the Sun) / 18
Letter to J.R. (Self Seen as Art 1) / 19

Two:

Letter to Miss Kim (We Prepare to Take Flight) / 23
Letter to J.R. (I Started a Life) / 24
Letter to Miss Kim (I Wait to Send Myself Home) / 25
Letter to J.R. (In Which I Surrender) / 26
Letter to Miss Kim (Pattern of Trees) / 27
Letter to J.R. (I Appeal to My Unfinished Hero) / 28
Letter to Miss Kim (Put On a New Body) / 30
Letter to J.R. (The Thought Salmon) / 32
Letter to Miss Kim (Light is So Long) / 34

Letter to J.R. (Self Seen as Art 2) / 35
Letter to Miss Kim (I Dim the Barometer) / 36
Letter to J.R. (The Love of Very Minor Detail) / 37
Letter to Miss Kim (Ticking Mechanical Wind Siren) / 38
Letter to J.R. (After Skimming Yin off the River Acheron) / 39
Letter to Miss Kim (I, Like the Asparagus) / 40

Three:
Letter to J.R. (To the Conch from Which a Gentle Light Sounds) / 43
Letter to Miss Kim (Saving You Safe in Mind) / 45
Letter to J.R. (I Explain a Few Things) / 46
Letter to Miss Kim (I Lament a Few Things) / 48
Letter to J.R. (Self Seen as Art 3) / 49
Letter to Miss Kim (Bottomless Cup) / 50
Letter to J.R. (When I'm Ready to Think of Something Else) / 51
Letter to Miss Kim (May the May Continue) / 52
Letter to J.R. (Self Seen as Art 4) / 53
Letter to Miss Kim (It Is a Terrarium) / 55
Letter to J.R. (A Bridge Spanning the Sleep of Earth) / 56
Letter to Miss Kim (A Foreign-Born Gardener) / 58

Four:

Letter to J.R. (Andrew Jackson Rides Again) / 61

Letter to Miss Kim (O, Unfamiliar Grove) / 66

Letter to J.R. (Someone Tonight is Knitting) / 68

Letter to Miss Kim (Keeping it Here for You) / 70

Letter to J.R. (Self Seen as Art 5) / 71

Letter to Miss Kim (If Not Beside Me) / 73

Letter to Miss Kim (Informal Invitation to a Traveler) / 74

Epilogue / 75

Notes / 78

The Only Day

Start with weather,
evaluate. Today
is hot. Today is
cold. One day
doesn't cause the next
Flowers bloom, Miss Kim,
the next day wilt,
burning to no benefit

Say it is cyclical,
say it renews itself:
today there were
accidents & tomorrow too
Another leaf on
last year's leaves
the ground under
inches of leaves
This the only honor this
life

One

Every Day the Little Arts Are Dying

Irreversibly strange are the heroes here.
They are always standing,
their hands rubbing out a quiet mumbling.
Their clothes heavier somehow,
like a marble bird stationed on each shoulder.

Scalpel winds tense edges of the water.
The cottage pipes bump and rock.
When the rain comes, I watch the river bulging,
drinking herself to unthinkable size.
Think of my mother—her mojitos
as the dryer ran, a room away.

But I have you now, J.R., and the rubbles of the cities
seem not so bad. The sea salt bathes
in the city of the dead. A sleepy logic overcomes
everything, we think, in the overpriced cafes where we sit.
And find such things occluded—time in its meander
turning each thought scarlet then cinder in turn.
Though we know it is good that we grasp at such
only as an afterthought.
Then the compass of our being swings west.

This Disaster Area

Hurricane of
traveler of
above & around, dark
middle of

heights and arrows, landings
& loading docks empty
vans empty trees
& mailboxes.

Miss Kim, each of us a fuselage
above and above or landed
& docked. You I
can't locate

Shorn & stubby field
corn harvested field with
snow. Your missing
fuselage in the sunrise

the place where you
crashed shines
without

The Three Storms

A person could go so many lives
strung along by the lingering actions of others—
the mother, the scholar,
the horny beast humping the houseplant.

I've always been a wind turning
through a telescope, a tablet carved from lightning.
The solicitous faces that surround me,
the no-man's land mounting between myself
and the inenviable.

Then the inevitable
light strikes a metronome in my drawing room.
A person could go her whole life thinking,
"The conflict of my time is this time,"
and drop dimes in a dog-shaped bank.
To pass it off solely as animal
is to forget the frozen red of berries
as they round the mouth and enter.

I know you are happiest
drinking from a daffodil's vase,
that microbes molded the world
as we believe it. The sky-drawn boundaries,
these ingenious seeds seen by night.
The sickly archer, the succubi

streamed into outcrop and byway by morning
are absent.

Walt says the self is three storms.
He says: "Begin by knowing
your body, all its fire, since birth is one.
And the hurricane that came that day
over the ill-written clouds
where a man was severing one wood to two,
green and glad in the mid-light,
was only your gratitude to have been.
And all you have learned since then is this,
is your loneliness—the axe of hardship in your hand,
the pack of stars on your back."

Renew Each Day with a Match

Daylight burns the corn
my machinations
work well in the heat & oil
in the fields
from the road passers pass
& drive. My duty to you is to rely
and be reliable
to gain passage between cows
the bright life around them
like a campfire
the way it never runs dry

If One Could Forget Katmandu

It is difficult, this emerging alone
from the dry-docked sub at the science center.
The halogen lights count backwards,
sleep crackles and sets across the city.

And there are isolations, J.R.
There's this illumination
of exits, a measure of wind
into which to merge.

The locals' houses I pass are butterflies:
airy and warm with the flitting life
of the interior. Even at a distance,
eating mapo doufu in the dim booth,
I can't help but feel the congenial energy
of the arena surrounding.

Clean a coffee stain from your shirt,
march into the avenue.
You associate adoration with a smell,
with a white-walled diner,
its unblemished shepherd's sky.

But why this?
Why not the lunar module?
Why not the locked apartment

where a girl turns
hands to tambourines,
hair to gold?

To Stand and Face the Face of the Sun

The high season
outside white hot
rails rest
Courtyard's chipped tiles
chipmunks & crows
hesitate to stand
The cars shimmer
and the grasses with heat
We on the street
hover & carry
through the operation
A thin air around us,
the reason

Self Seen as Art 1

The grass is many baubles
stacked against each other,
and today you will not leave the beloved.
You will see a man,
your friend, wearing his Amish hat,
his grey suit, pointing to a lot
where a president's mother gave birth.

The laundry rapping blindly
against the air. The leaves
burgeoned brown.
Is this pump-handle hose,
this perfect terrace of opals
worth missing this shadow
bled lovely onto the lawn?

Tell it to the marionette shades,
Charon, and the children—
not pictured here—lounging
in the gangling, arboreal arms.
Tell it to me when I have begun
the end of my bloom,
wilt into water, ask to thirst.
Put on my Sunday shoes.
Tell it to me as I tell you:
my finger in the air.

The chickens, I point.
The pregnant barn
dampening the lamplight.

Two

We Prepare to Take Flight

Wind a straight line
unless redirected, unless

a fan or corner or tree
sends it slingshot

As much as any
leaf or dry grass

on this wind I move
on chance. The wind

without wanting
carries me

it doesn't mind and
doesn't know I was

for a while with.

I Started a Life

The wind between branches, the littered bits of atmosphere
outside the glass factory began to fade.
And for an eight-year old, I was a freighter
vanishing into violet light.
Then the sun dyed dark. An aunt took her home.
And when she woke again, the flowers
were hats tilted unevenly. Rain collected longing.
Sidewalk cracks, sixteen years in the making, made,
and worms, worried for drowning, slept to the surface.

We, the crew and I, watched the Nephilim arrange the sky,
turning some stars, extinguishing others. The waves
away from shore, livid ribbons, and, magic,
you ceded so little in eleven years adrift.

But where is the weight of abandoning held for you, J.R.?
The barrel of the eye? Wings extended over fields, dams?
Or is memory let to pellets, bits of shriek and bone,
indigestible even in recognition of need?

I hear the wind's seeds.
I hear the unsleeping pipes happy to be little but harbingers.
The tone deaf pipes of the city speak
misheard Thomas from skyscraper to sky—
And after this death, we could not die.

I Wait to Send Myself Home

A birth into another
precise word
lavender, crocus

we don't know
each other, voices
through walls

wall of wind, wall of
mind, me from
me, across the

river is a corresponding
solution, this mathematics

of continuing
as if the same

In Which I Surrender

Most often, our pain's at half-mast.
Against our will, hoisted down, turned to triangles,
incinerated. While whatever's outside grief goes on.
Salt and beef in the cellar, bats aggregating in the roofs.
An untidy universe refracted back to the eye by steel.

As if mastery of the body were our most accomplished lie.
And divides a woman from man in sleep and storm
and in the child's thunder in the early morning,
the boom of it nearly invited.

The colossus mountain shadows in a window.
The isolating messiness of children
from the lawn has vanished. Where,
in night, one sees through slitted eyes
the grass of mice bending.
As if this were a visitation.
The wound O of a tree branch let go,
the whump of it sounded in the air.

Pattern of Trees

Out of nowhere night
came through the pipes.
I saw my reasons for being here
without you in the leaves
Rebuilt, I'll find some
ground for morning.
Every single tree
is busted.

I Appeal to My Unfinished Hero

A brief hypnosis brought on by deer clipping leaves from the
forest skirt,
and when you come out of it, your sneakers are gone.
Someone's pinned two wings to a shirt, your shirt.

You feel today as if the poses you've assumed so unnaturally
might have been of some greater significance after all.

Like a monk who's been handed down the holy relic,
you eat of the toaster pastry and irradiate orange juice.
While I spend my hours parsing out your most minor acts.

Why you'll think to yourself
(metro train entering the black breath of the tunnel),
"The absence of love's our only measure of it,"
and how I will save you from yourself. And how for either of us
it will only be a thing to have happened
and clipped on windward.

Somewhere, a barfly spreads his arms and legs
and the archeologist uncovers the impression of a body burned
away.

Every reflected light off a barb or the winsome barn before I exit
the highway
dreams me back to this moment

when we sit outside the convenience store and I say,

"You can't run from your Ninevehs forever."
And you say, "Take your arm off my arm."

And I think,
"Even the rusted-out spade of the heart has its purpose."

Put On a New Body

Face masks the common population
put yours on & horrify

to go out shrouded
a necessary armor

complicated insides
remain inside

(tearing into
wormy interior
of mice &
canisters of fur)

those remaindered
in the prairie grass
& those still moving

I look into each one
look for you
look into my own

it is difficult
to see

the cold, the fight
the aging light

requires

The Thought Salmon

No one need instruct me on the reasoning for suffering
just as no one need explain the salmon
who fell from the sky.

Remain behind the yellow line,
we were asked. But our thoughts
rubbed at patio windows,
they barked at odd hours.
There was a rustle in the undergrowth;
afterward our thoughts were absent altogether.
Gazing on our freshly raspberried bushes,
only a cup of tea occupied us.

A short time after, the salmon died,
and our thoughts eventually returned. Slowly
and unsurely, tails tucked between their legs.
Thoughts of diaphanous fauna;
children frozen to dipods in the park;
the colossus who wanders your world
and taps the saints to sleep.
Thoughts of optical effects,
imaginings seen in Tupperware;
then the salmon, who'd appeared again.
The sink this time.

A thought begins in the wild,

said the salmon, *and lures us by bits of bread.*
When we arrive at its cottage,
we may smell a scent of sugar and incense.
It may lay a coarse hand across our shoulder.

In those days, you could watch yourself
as a cowl and haircut bobbing along an avenue.
You could hear anyone
wondering on what mercy was.

And was it out of mercy
that the salmon ascended?
At funerals,
they say take off your hat,
but no one is wearing a hat.
So, you tap your head where you think
a thought might muster.
You imagine a bugle is blown.

Light is So Long

Longest day, armed for violence
will I never see you
in my new home

to the floor, to the window
to the tree dead amid the
blooming

trees unlit amid
the green torches & bombs
of blossoms you

decline to answer
decline   you
more noticeable
in your absence

Self Seen as Art 2

A whole block burns down in Munich,
and someone at a train station
grafitis Goodnight Shoes
onto the train trellis.
Goodnight knotted track.
Clay light. Whisky sky
which overtakes even the dust
beyond the boundaries of the camp.

So long, horizon of tarp. So long,
eruptive smoke. Dantean cliffs, abridge
what's below. Wind on toward town
primered by lightning. You speak in croaks,
storm, not in numbers. So long!
I saw the long-tailed d you scripted,
and I did my days wandering the waste,
and I saw the melted windows.
Out January, I grappled in bars
and when I spoke, I spoke solemnly—
a voice over an intercom.

I Dim the Barometer

Cold gentle my water
lay on the table
like so much fabric

you drink your life
try morning   so long

as the clouds march
and build
a pressure
the storm
its quick demands

tell me again
tell me again what's
so long taste

The Love of Very Minor Detail

Running hands through hair, remove from your lips a pearl.
Your head on a cushion makes another head
saying something quite different.

At least, this is how the blimp driver pictures our lives.
Below, between us is the unwashed cup of time. One of us,
whose failure to empty the lint trap has not gone unnoticed,
dreams dreams one freeze-dries in absence of their other.
Things like that.

There's the café in Mount Vernon, its spirits,
carrot cake which costs more than a tank of gas.
When you pay what's asked,
when you walk away to where there's little town left.
A cloud paves the horizon
so one hand's a glove. Then, by wind,
five fingers, two rings, a scepter.

Out Akron, and the trees-of-heaven
plant evidence along the highway.

Ticking Mechanical Wind Siren

A tree falls
on the house
& also the fence
It takes hours
for the blood, for the
wrapping, for the cutting
for the saving
Meantime the sirens
Meantime the aftermath
I can see very clearly
despite injuries
I still have structure

After Skimming Yin off the River Acheron

It's no small thing,
the truck who mauled a deer uneasily asleep at the roadside.
This bald light you drink from the clock tower
and how these cow-spotted petunias
impinge to nothing your anger.

Each day, high-rises could crush you
(their restless budding) if not for your heaving laugh
which fogs over the executive's view.

And it's no small thing that your voice in my ear
resembles a baton thrown to the air. Go see.
The sea is spotted and breaks.
Our neighbors were once our friends.

Against my bedspread, your plumage made an autumn
weave. But how could I begrudge you your rest?
As you stretched,
a radiologic star shone out of the sky
and I felt you might never leave.

And it's no small thing
that you told me once of a fruit eaten only in the Orient
knowing full well these feral hands who stalk the grounds
and the many lives I would leave
to meet you.

I, Like the Asparagus

A swamp comes in
it is Florida today
the plants, happy
the envelopes stick to each other
I stick to me, carry myself heavy

The swelter worsens
turns us all to food
not a friend or a wanted

How clumsy, personal
to be a sun,
lean down,
empty charge account over
a limp everything

Three

To the Conch from Which a Gentle Light Sounds

There was Knife and there was Candle, who lived in the blue house by the dark-skinned cherry trees. Candle out on the veranda, Knife calling her name from the street. Knife in plaid pants running the mulcher. Sometimes Candle laughing to herself while Knife swore the spa to a hail of nuts and bolts.

Knife loved the smell of Candle fallen from her hair—its inviting, tender air and always the something of her whereabouts imbedded. A humid linen from the laundromat, talc from a friend's gymnasium. The hair was Knife's Scheherazade and each night he gathered its gifts to his touch.

In the morning, Knife settles over his paper—his ex-wife has died. Candle pouring Corn Pops in a bowl. Her southern accent, sudden awareness of the bloodlessness of his arms. Candle scoots around the chair, puts the spoon to her mouth. What's wrong? she asks.

Down in the cellar, they are digging in the dust-sticky cardboard. Here, says Candle. They flip through photos, Knife explaining each one. Knife flipping forward. Candle flipping backward. Knife cutting the cake, his wife's nose smeared with wet frosting. That cabin on the lake in the town with its thousand novelty flags.

What were you like? asks Candle.

Miserable mostly.

Be honest, she says.

We lived by burnt-out television, the white-hot arguments. Always one of us misunderstood by the other, then the fuming, yelling, usual makeup.

Look at this one, says Candle. She steps back holding a wrinkled letter.

They go upstairs. She sets Knife to rest on the couch, and when she comes back from the recycling bin, he's asleep again. She stoops to caress his head. Light lines his body and the burnet hairs of his arm.

Oh Knife, in this two-horse town, what can one do but rest? And a gate, long ivied over, parts in Knife's chest.

Saving You Safe in Mind

I was going to say
move slowly beside
the others so
elbows & raw bricks
won't uproot you since you
the same way as the plants
are dependent on me
remembering. Keys & location
change when I'm not
looking, little grasses
sprouting late in the season
Centuries of old life
grown over everybody's
doing a brand new dance now.

I Explain a Few Things

Sometimes it happens that the Invisible Hand
moves a bar graph of bulls from one continent
to another. At other times, one of Fate's hands
delivers a flat brush into an artist's waiting hand.
A star forms in the cobalt autumn,
and soon one stares down virtuosity
in the wealthy art houses of the city.

Sometimes, though, one hand brushes the other
as the two pass over the Eastern Seaboard
or the Sea of Sargasso. The Invisible Hand
might skim the hem of Fate's dress
when the two are walking in the garden
of a mutual friend. *I hear the Outerbanks
are best this time of year*.

It's a curious thing—
how in one town we might be burning the monster,
and the next, find ourselves listening to tides
through their discarded adornments.
There are many precarious chambers through which
the inner music must weave.

Beyond the low, wet tresses, servants pull
peat from the earth. The hand of Fate perches,
at times, in the low-lying branches of the estate.

The Invisible Hand riding bareback
the New England lanes. A traveler passing such a night
might see the unveiled face of commerce.
She might hear a sigh or sound like one wave waxing,
intruding on another.

I Lament a Few Things

A long time ago
beneath the sour desert
as if we weren't interested
we lived

For now
this is what we get

Frozen aquifers,
trick heart
repairs
of icy lines

To do over what we did
To do over what we did

Self Seen as Art 3

The darkness visible but by water
clots into continents, waits.
A headstrong moon speaks itself
into the greening deep, divides the skiff
from what fleets and flows.

The boat leaves creases, imprecise images—
portraits the water is obligated to render.
This sky's inhalation settles
damp on the rigging. There is Peter,
the rock, indecision, devotion.
How we arrive in port
more minor than imagined.

What is the world if not these waves,
this opacity greeting our ends?
I understand *The darkness around us
is deep* one means as more than metaphor.
A spume is one such miracle. The Christ
indiscernible from the seaspray and mist about him.
He is singing the oldest man's sea song
distant from the darkened glade.

Bottomless Cup

I scrub salt off the steps
succumb to weather
& growth spurts

Daily I climb a billion flights of stairs

You drink from a well of endless
sweet water   endless refill

Miss Kim, you ask me
for another cup
and I am on a blank sea
keening

for I am responsible for you
I am neglectful of you
wherein lies
the faith of the scenario

When I'm Ready to Think of Something Else

I think we've tackled this sundown
with the smallness of our ideas.
I've made a mess
of red mites in my books;
you've written the alphabet
of omission. One can barely stand the television
when the sun bristling like a lake calls.

See, what's sacred also burns.
Like the prayer candles at Mont. St. Michel.
And, at certain times, a child strips a relic
from a sanctuary
while the monk's world paces
and alters immeasurably—
Jeroboam and his skin-tight denim,
new tunes on the air.

We record over wedding videos by accident.
The drooping tulip does without us.
Stare at the stain glass landscape; it cows us!
Then turns inaccessible like this present
and the next. And so fragile,
our victories. So bright, the crumbs
you eat from St. Michael's steps.

May the May Continue

The Spring is dead long live the Spring
long live the buds long live
the sun resting on the
leaves at the angle
just into our eyes
like epiphany
long live blue sky
long live new geese new deer
new nests secure in the tree of new life

Self Seen as Art 4

A deep blue settles to the bottom
of a relic made by a recluse
for a woman
who did not love him.
What resembles, but is not solely, a clock.

I envision the tiny apes
who occupy its cogs.
Their lives off center stage
spent writing up reports.
Harrow
an instruction manual in anxiety.
Why didn't I study design?
sighs one ape.

Then the director lifts his wand,
their instruments ascend to their sternums.
And it is Friday, and maybe
you could believe love.
At least a little.

And do. A rich royal blue
decks the balcony above the opera house
where, waiting at arm's length,
you enwrap
in the eyes of the amorous one.

Free from all else
(yourself)
if only for this instant.

Your sole song. So long
odious modesty. So long
since this slow light,
and October
failing all around you.

It Is a Terrarium

I stop am
stopped & go
if allowed

it is a
terrarium
glass walls amplify
& produce

if an echo
comes in
it stays & I sing
to it. I respond

& respond
& am—am I—

I am
what hits
me & what
I live with

A Bridge Spanning the Sleep of Earth

Moon, you play your barren harp above the world,
a wastebasket out of which you eat Oreos.
I've written many a rock-lullaby in our time apart.
I am playing one such song presently.
Out on the veranda,
Moon, you fall into another drink.
I lean to tune to the ear, for all the good ideas
anyone had are still out there.
Would you consider yourself "an antler?"
At each incremental advance of technology
there is a brief juncture where the wicked
simply outpace us, the armed populace.
But each utters the same ritual to you, Moon.
Let's say you and I burn these old goat bones together.
Yesterday, I saw you. You lay in the park—grass
groveling in and over you. The children stole your head,
your iron and aluminum head,
then lost interest, left you to ants, sand.
From the car, I could clearly see your sigh
as you counted each step back across
the words of the poem in which you were.
When your sigh reached me, I tuned my little e to it.
You say, Come try your act out by the custom house.
And I come. I play that aged love song of yours.
Twist out old rags. Learn to punch
the snack machine just so. Though, you know,

some unlucky contingent dies each year
over eighty cents of snacks. People leave their lives for less.
You said, Come play your barren harp above the world.
And I wept. And now everyone in town calls me at odd hours;
dragging my good name through the dust.

A Foreign-Born Gardener

Tough to break and correspond
to break & listen those people
the walls and where will I
everyone moving go

The day—an animal—a rabid
although time   there is no
to break and lean
palms on the overhang
to weave them dry
& leave them strewn

a distance
flinging me
strangely populated plot

Four

Andrew Jackson Rides Again

I.

The hardware has broken, J.R.
Its fedora has fallen, its toupee slumps.
The rats run from its side,
their grumbling limbs rumbling the slums.

Yesterday, I witnessed a face in a mirror
form from powder. A face drummed into mist and lost
while the stockbrokers pissed in their train station
shifting quarter from pocket to hand.
Ill-mannered, they exited this place.

Where gravity vibrates a little too cumbrous,
where a line at a bakery becomes electric.
Sex occurs. Deer enter.
A question of mortality asks of us.

And from the bedside where the harp of alarms string,
I'm not attentive enough to answer.
Nor can I be certain how to cease feeling
as one holding a leash in rain. Hopeful, anxious,
ill-equipped for the physical life in its marvel.

I lurch through the lime-soft streets.
The mirrored face recurs on a girl

encased in a coral cloud of dress
who lifts her hem slightly,
races from one engagement to another.

Hardware, beyond your high-rise an eclipse
dons its lusterless wings. Your children,
witless, scattered, operate their calendars.
In your daughter's home, the silver
is always in perfect arrangement,
the phone is always ringing.

Electric crosses angle down where the sewer sows its waste.
Caskets of eggs. Bubble wrap lured into manholes.

And though Andrew Jackson rides beside me now,
always at the edge of tearing,
where we're going they'll be no more need for presidents.
Milkweed in a ditch, hands stripping a head
of wheat. The crowds, the smoke, a flued scent of new asphalt.

Huzzah to the end of wiretaps, sings Jackson!
Huzzah to the ceasing of the criminal modes
done the backbone of the common man!

Jackson pulls up a sleeve. He dredges wishes from fountains.
He huffs his snuff. His eyes are white dwarfs wasting dusk
to nothing. To stand before him is to bear the roc
of a million grave days. Oh, the empire of him is a gavel!
Oh, the roc's feathers smash our skulls!

II.

Unscrupulous are the gods by whom the ancients swore.
And I admit, I want the great laden past to know
my name also. I want Olympus to shoot its silver arrow
into this overgrown grass.

But the unaccounted histories have long now
undertaken their odyssey to decay. A middle-aged man
smoking over a trout. Above the greening bay,
light and cloud the color of fish gut.
Smog, winter-raw limbs,
delinquents lifting paint to stain a billboard.
Was this the conquest as envisioned?
I've forgotten some hundred times the mission.
I say my piece to the high flames of the synagogue.
Hills of apartments, each with its gouged out eye.

It seems a satellite-distant shot of an island now—
even primates escaped earth before us.
Our pride allowed it. Our scotch fostered it.
The water cooler became our sanctuary.

Jackson, my improvised hero, aid me!
But someone has canoed across his heart.
A kettle of blood rings in his head.
He will begin again. Composing his will

by the phosphorescent subways,
the since blown pilot lights of stars.
His verse will make us to miss our fellows again.
It must, he says.

I imagine a video run in reverse of the fisherman's catch.
Air exits the lungs, the stomach floods again with hope.
The ox-colored eyes open against the silt, the pull.
From the surface, a hangman's rope.

III.

The warlike present will not be altered.
Not abacas enough to count these off-almond skies,
the grey dragoons settled on the grass.
The billion-some brown napkins—
catalogs of "things to do today"— I unfurl at times.
Wishes washed from life to death:
"Listen to Lisa," "Oil bill off tomorrow."

Gullible moon. The long-suffering wives of the stars are here.
Vacant deer bodies mottled by rocks line the highways.

I will tell you a true thing:
no one would consent to see it all.

Optimism, this thin brightness
by which oil baron, seamstress,

strong-willed wanderers bore on.

Jackson dreams an uncle, wounded once
with a hunting musket, plays a flute in the high grass.
Andrew runs to the marsh, but he's old again.
A frog yearns up at him from the morass.
And then nothing. No street trolled to life by vehicle, no silo.

The hardware taps out its survival on my marrow.
I tap back, "There were some apples left upon a bough"—
but the rest is lost to distance.
Because little changes. Because anything of real substance
must change. Because I was many years
the soil's slave and ride, now, comported far from it.
And admire much and miss little, but Jackson in his sleep
whose hand is shaking. Whose hand is this whole planet's
shaking.
Whose eye opens lightning from a cloud.
And the heavy rains that wake us and the high, haughty clouds
who are laughter.

O, Unfamiliar Grove

Miss Kim, you—
Miss Kim, we—
Berries on branches

regardless of season. I look
for buds and mislead myself in looking
It is never Spring, it

barren and cold, no
fresh fields or fertilizers
I look for the absence

and negative because what
is here is too hard
Frozen ground. Frozen branches

Frozen worms stranded from a storm
of misleading rain
To be precise about it:

your memory has changed
Do you remember how
you used to feel on the street

in town in the sun
when you saw

without conviction, which was luxury

And what you must do
what you cannot resist doing
is want, and to feel it cold

within. This is the Kim
you are, this is who—
a new cold wind once I think it over

Someone Tonight Is Knitting

Dear Adonic Others,

Know we are cheering you
when your hair falls
or you squeeze
thoughts through a mail slot.
Files can't be recovered,
and your brother is very ill,
and at any minute
this whole deal could go.

Go. And if you become
what is asked,
it was not felicity.
A mother of two
and the two,
who have treated the neighbor's rental
to death by muddy shoes,
love which will not reprimand
it was not. Anything of awe
which saved you.

Dear Adonic Others,

Search for your screws
by one working lamp.
You descend
to the grand disguise party
that is Death.
This clacking of needles
from without or withal.

From your hall,
the light left by two lives
twines in air.

Dear Sweethearts,

Dear Exoskeletons,

Know we want to have wanted for you
what was
best. For you,
the smallest thought
may string
incalculable hours.

Dear Brevities,
Dear Dear and Distant,
Dear Cauldron of Rain,

Keeping it Here For You

Out of hard ground we
were born, not soil
Tiny trees only poles
and orange berries

Now weather approaching,
fields bloom dirt
it's alright it's dark
to the left

gates dried open
all night to welcome
dust garlic blooms
onion blooms tubers

torn & knit through screens
on the porch, old porch
where we would sit

Self Seen as Art 5

And I've tried to think the right things, J.R.

The laggard dream
of summer sloping into the valley.
Returning to see the farmer,
found only his house, his ox.

The ox's hoof slips
as she steps
over the track that parts
the long wheat pasture
from the blackhanded hills.

I imagine the farmer's children.
Their Sundays
of incommunication.

I watch the hands
drawing
them from the dark hill,
their xylem, phloem
hair snipped short.

You quaff the stars
for you believe in them
you have life.

Move out to the porch,
its pillars
so many muscled hands.

And I think on this ivory magic
we've been
wielding, you and I.

These faces in the sheen off the moon
on the truck, and I am tired of dreaming
says the sun to the stars. Of the tiny shapes
who look upon me. And sometimes one will scrape.
And sometimes one will sigh.

If Not Beside Me

Closing the interstate, the attic
taping the windows shut
each day here & you
and I'm afraid like ____
and about to ____
avalanches inside &
out the invisible
monsters, how places, how I'm
aluminum & caravans
of trucks   snows   waves

Informal Invitation to a Traveler

Will I have a visitor or will I
not or will I
be sleeping and forsake a traveler
I cannot wait this way
cannot wait for you my house
who is untidy
who has no lemons
little twigs all over
blown in from all over
what will it mean
for winter here
I must rebuild
within myself
the home that lasts

Epilogue (To Be a Part)

There's a city where the street's a light. Where the windows into light unlatch and out of their mouths come moths. The moths stream the roads causing passersby to swat and dance, drop a cantaloupe.

In this city, the people vanish into light and saunter out of light. Sometimes living one life, sometimes another. It's possible, in the city, to fall asleep in lingerie and snap back to consciousness, to a spreadsheet at a desk where you work. One person boards an aircraft, another emerges, back stiff, a breath of stale pretzels. In the dampness of the airport's florescence they say to each other, "Do you ever wish we'd have night? Like two big waters could push light from light and end up with something else."

But they don't mean it, these people. Don't blame them; their ideas are little pouches of sand poured, all their days, into a desert.

In this city, the choir boys carry my coffin to the center of town. Four basalt pillars are set and my coffin shouldered atop it. One boy wipes his head with his hat and they shuffle off, hands in pockets, kicking a clod of earth. It wasn't sad, knowing I would die. All day the light's a goat and little girl laughing. They rattle and snort, one pulling the other by lasso. I see auroras, flashes of a woman's earring falling unnoticed in the fountain. Children kick a ball beneath me. A shadow emits, and their acceptance of it seems all I ever asked.

I've understood enough of the path to know I've lived a thorn.
When I was eight, a mineshaft became my mother. I grew
ragged, unaffected, all relatives dead of revolution or alcohol.
Some boy came to take my book and I killed him. They were
right to hang me, bury me in the shallow bog, and that I've
arrived here— sitting on a stone, my huntsmen's gown half-
digested—seems right too.

To return to this single reality, then to be the dark moment of a
moth's wings, defines for me the impossible. We learn to love in
spite of the shade we proffer or foster discontent to an art.
Though by neither am I made sufficient, the silence of this
music's also music. I allow it to take me to the city's square
where the short politician shouts from his stacked bread racks.
To its effortless untenability by which I am certain of its truth.
It's feeling of a dress slipped over a neck and the crack of
hunters in the outliers and the lighted windows

in which they sleep.

Notes

"Self Seen as Art 1" is from Grant Wood's "The Birthplace of Herbert Hoover."

"Self Seen as Art 2" is from Ansiem Keifer's "Untitled."

"Self Seen as Art 3" is from Henry Osawa Tanner's "The Disciples See Christ Walking on the Water."

"Self Seen as Art 4" is from Joseph Cornell's "Untitled (Pour Valery)."

"Self Seen as Art 5" is from Edward Hopper's "American Landscape 1920."

A special thanks to editors. Poems from this manuscript were featured in:

Catch-Up: Letter to Miss Kim (Keeping it Here for You), Letter to Miss Kim (If Not Beside Me)

Columbia Poetry Review: Letter to J.R. (A Bridge Spanning the Sleep of Earth)

Devil's Lake: Letter to Miss Kim (I Wait to Send Myself Home), Letter to J.R. (Self Seen as Art 1)

Pismire Poetry: Letter to J.R. (Self Seen as Art 5), Letter to Miss Kim (May the May Continue)

Plaid Review: Letter to J.R. (I Explain a Few Things), Letter to J.R. (After Skimming Yin off the River Acheron)

Rougarou: Letter to J.R. (Self Seen as Art 3)

narrative (dis)continuities: prose experiments by younger american writers: Letter to J.R. (To the Conch From Which a Gentle Light Sounds), Letter to J.R. (To Be a Part)

Kyle McCord's first book, *Galley of the Beloved in Torment*, was the winner of the 2008 Orphic Prize and was released by Dream Horse Press. He has work forthcoming or published from *Boston Review, Columbia: a Journal of Art and Literature, Cream City Review, Gulf Coast, Painted Bride Quarterly, Volt,* and elsewhere. He's worked for *The Beloit Poetry Journal, jubilat,* and *The Nation*. Currently, he lives in Des Moines, Iowa where he coordinates The Younger American Poets Reading Series.

Jeannie Hoag was born in Wisconsin and is currently a librarian in Buffalo, New York. She is a graduate of the MFA Program for Poets & Writers at the University of Massachusetts, Amherst. Her chapbook New Age of Ferociousness was published in 2010 by Agnes Fox Press.